Math = Fun!™

Multiplication

2 × 3 = 6

by Jerry Pallotta
Illustrated by Rob Bolster

SCHOLASTIC INC.

New York   Toronto   London   Auckland   Sydney
Mexico City   New Delhi   Hong Kong   Buenos Aires

For the Bolivian Olivian!

—Jerry Pallotta

To Mr. DelSignore

—Rob Bolster

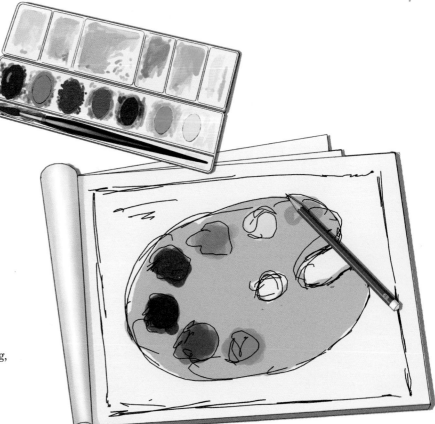

ISBN-13: 978-0-545-00686-6
ISBN-10: 0-545-00686-4

Text copyright © 2008 by Jerry Pallotta.
Illustrations copyright © 2008 by Rob Bolster.
All rights reserved. Published by Scholastic Inc.
SCHOLASTIC, MATH=FUN!, and associated logos
are trademarks of Scholastic Inc.

12 11 10 9 8 7 6 5 4 3   8 9 10 11 12 13/0

Printed in the U.S.A.
First printing, March 2008

**This is two books in one!
Learn about multiplication in a fun and easy way—
and learn about different techniques
for drawing and painting!**

Art times math equals fun.

1	2	3	4
5	6	7	8
9	10	11	12

How many sections are in this grid? You can count them—
one, two, three, four, five, six, seven, eight, nine, ten, eleven, and twelve.
But there is an easier way to find out the number of sections.
It is called multiplication.

This is a grid. Inside is an array of numbers. An array is a set of numbers arranged in order. Look for patterns.

	1	2	3	4	5	6	7	8	9	10	11	12	13	14	15
1	1	2	3	4	5	6	7	8	9	10	11	12	13	14	15
2	2	4	6	8	10	12	14	16	18	20	22	24	26	28	30
3	3	6	9	12	15	18	21	24	27	30	33	36	39	42	45
4	4	8	12	16	20	24	28	32	36	40	44	48	52	56	60
5	5	10	15	20	25	30	35	40	45	50	55	60	65	70	75
6	6	12	18	24	30	36	42	48	54	60	66	72	78	84	90
7	7	14	21	28	35	42	49	56	63	70	77	84	91	98	105
8	8	16	24	32	40	48	56	64	72	80	88	96	104	112	120
9	9	18	27	36	45	54	63	72	81	90	99	108	117	126	135
10	10	20	30	40	50	60	70	80	90	100	110	120	130	140	150

In math, this is the multiplication sign, or a times sign. It is used to multiply numbers.

Here is an equals sign. It is used in equations to show that two or more numbers are equal in value.

$$3 \times 4 = 12$$

In the art room,
the kids are drawing lines with pen and ink.

A grid is also drawn with lines. It is perfect to use when learning multiplication.
This grid has three sections in each vertical column
and four sections in each horizontal row. Three times four equals twelve.
We did not have to count every one of the sections. We multiplied.

1 × 1 = 1

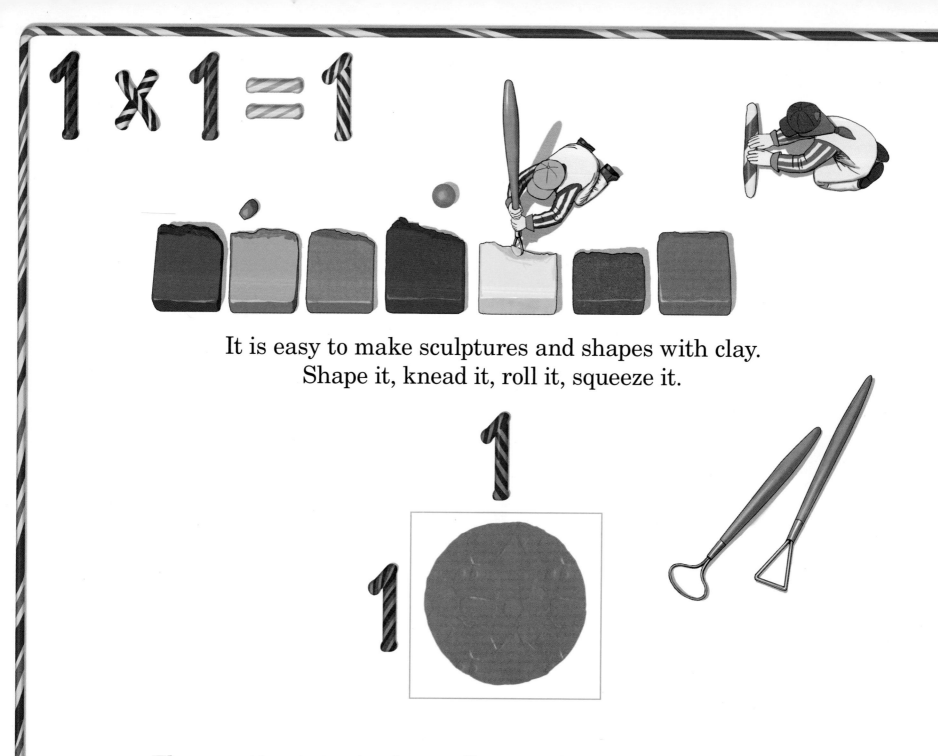

It is easy to make sculptures and shapes with clay.
Shape it, knead it, roll it, squeeze it.

The equation 1×1=1 is also really easy. One times one equals one.
If you take one thing, one time, you have one.

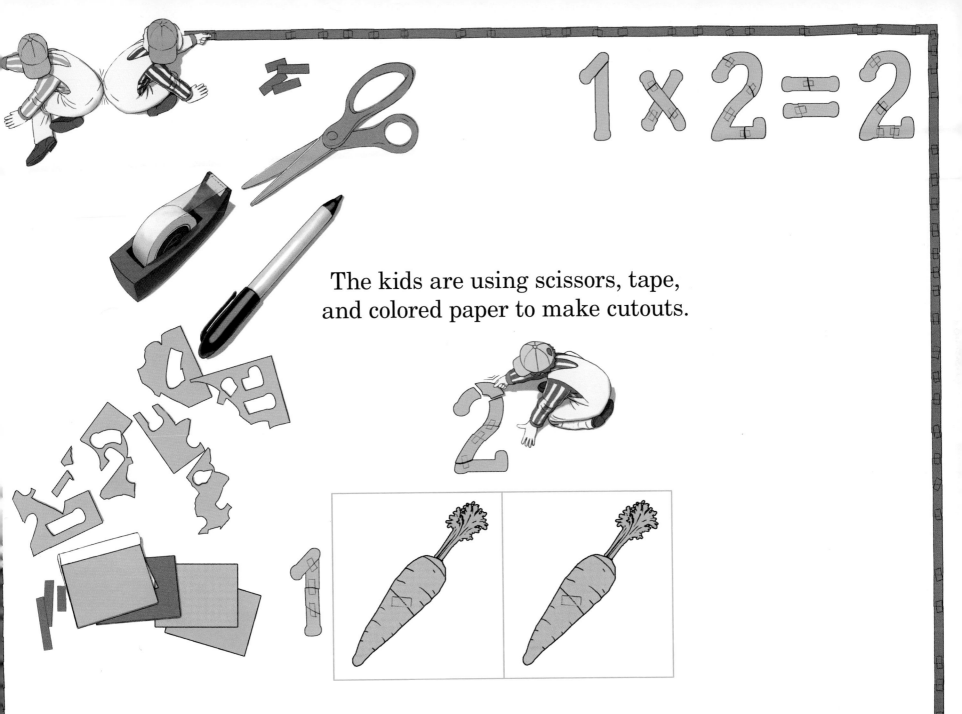

$$1 \times 2 = 2$$

The kids are using scissors, tape, and colored paper to make cutouts.

If you take one thing, two times, you have two!
One times two equals two.

1 x 3 = 3

It is time to paint with an airbrush, which is like a little spray gun.

Compressed air combines with paint to create a mist. Always point the spray away from your face.

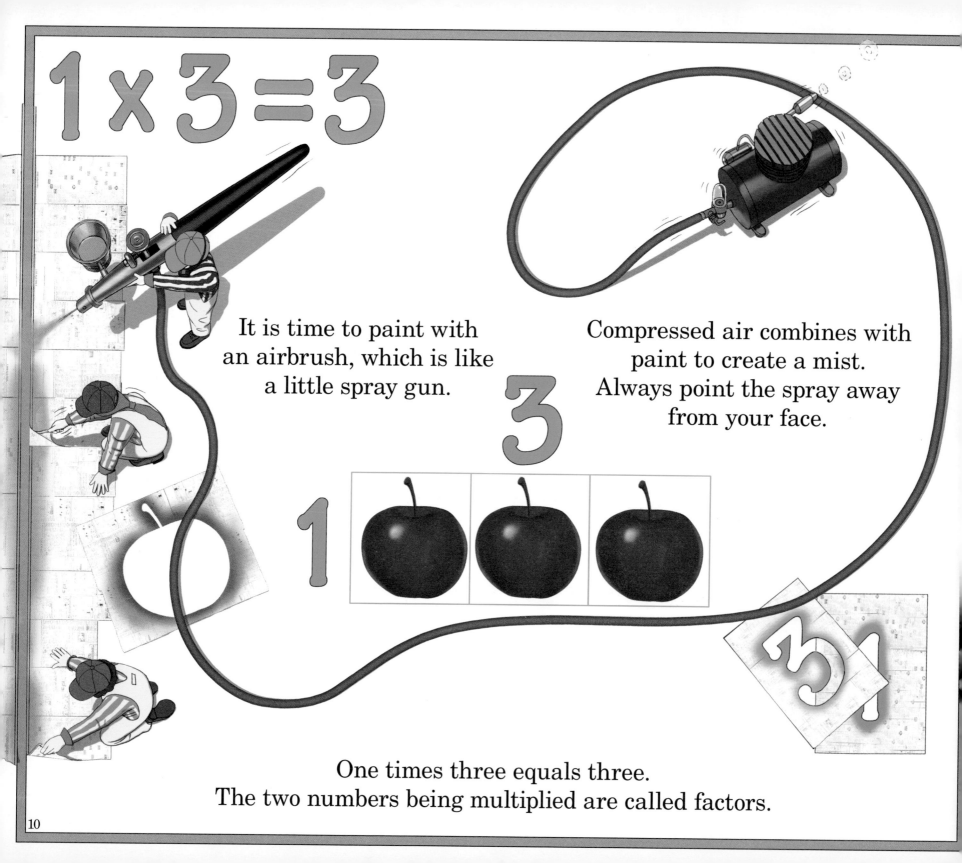

One times three equals three.
The two numbers being multiplied are called factors.

1 x 4 = 4

Hey, kids, be careful with the paints.
Don't forget to clean your brushes.

4

1

One times four equals four.
One times any factor equals that factor.
When doing multiplication, the answer is called the product.
A factor times a factor equals a product.

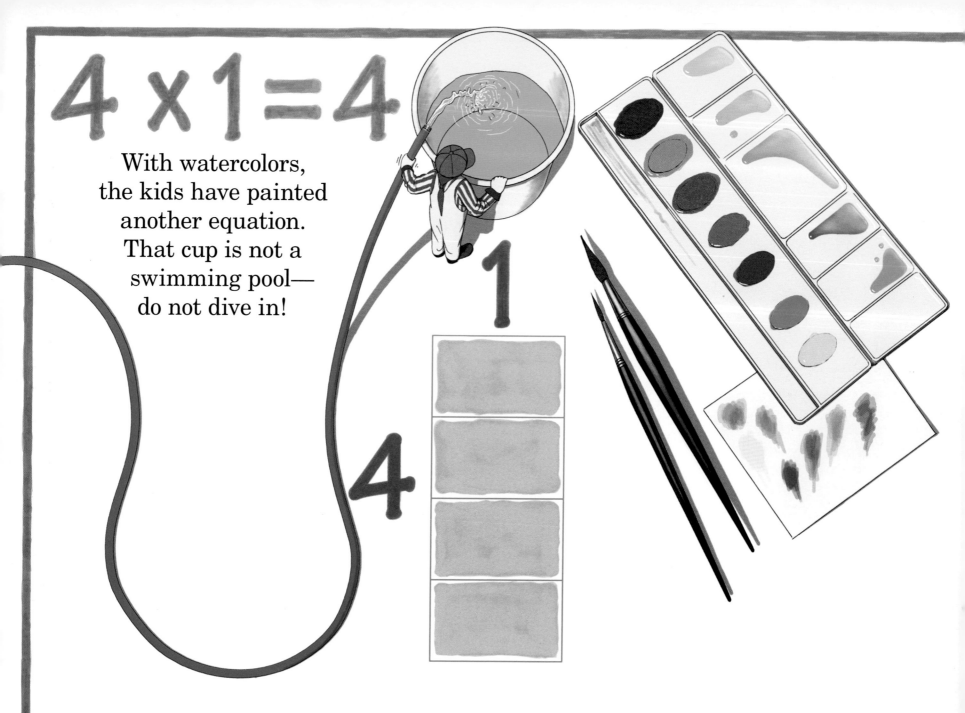

$4 \times 1 = 4$

With watercolors, the kids have painted another equation. That cup is not a swimming pool— do not dive in!

Horizontal equations like **4×1=4** go from side to side just like the horizon.
Four times one equals four.

The kids have colored an
equation using crayons.

$$\begin{array}{r} 3 \\ \times 1 \\ \hline 3 \end{array}$$

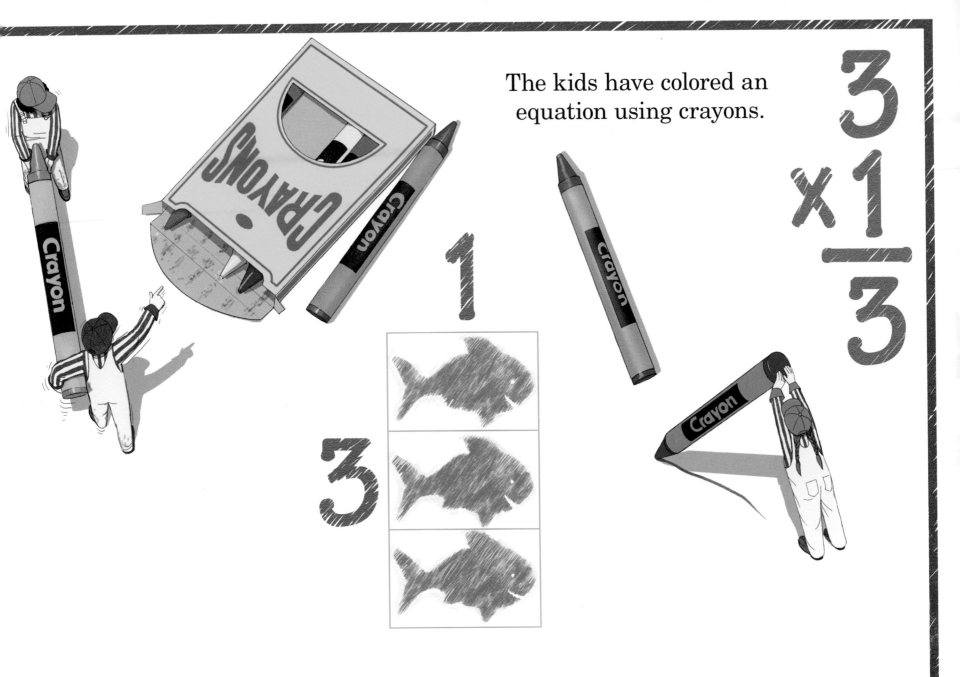

This page is a little different. This equation $\begin{array}{r} 3 \\ \times 1 \\ \hline 3 \end{array}$ is vertical.
This multiplication fact goes up and down instead of across.
Three times one equals three.

2 × 1 = 2

For a lighter, softer color, you can draw with pastels.

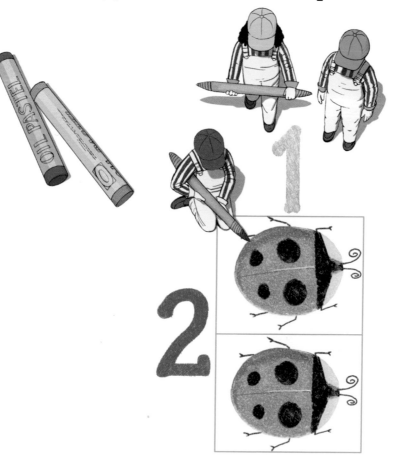

Numbers can be multiplied in any order.
If the two factors are reversed, the product is still the same.
Two times one equals two. One times two equals two.
This is called the commutative property of multiplication.

Beadwork is another way to create designs. Put the needle with thread through the hole in each bead and create your own border or necklace.

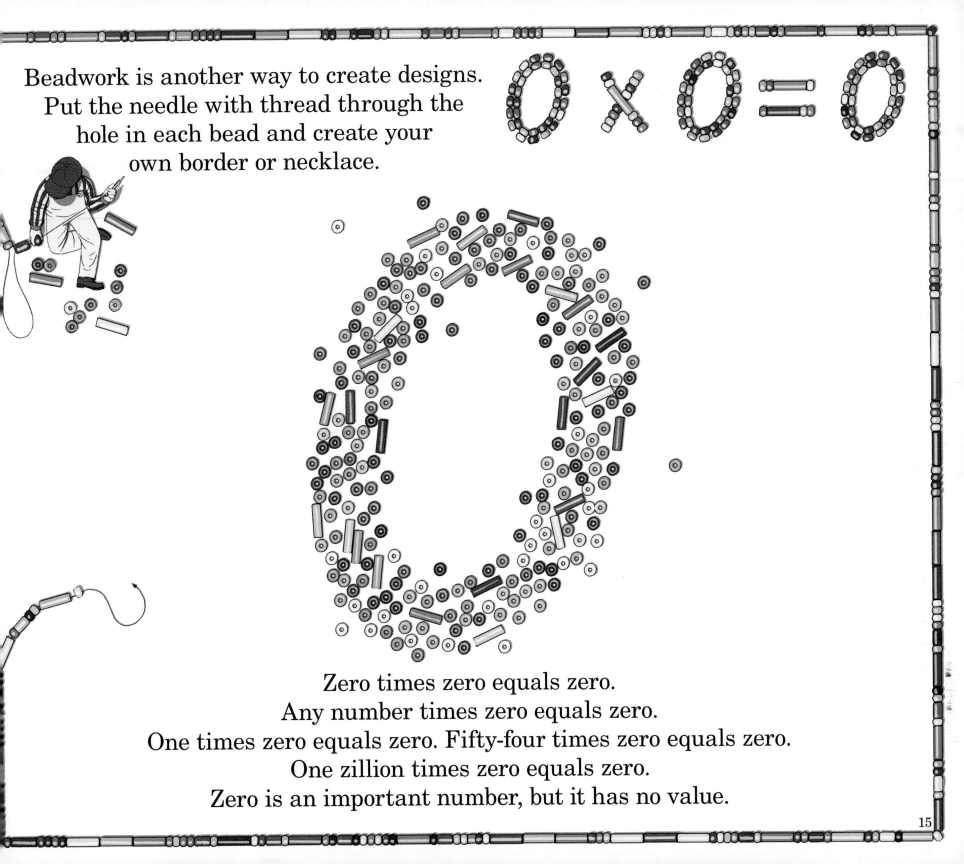

Zero times zero equals zero.
Any number times zero equals zero.
One times zero equals zero. Fifty-four times zero equals zero.
One zillion times zero equals zero.
Zero is an important number, but it has no value.

Basic Multiplication Facts

0×0=0	0×1=0	0×2=0	0×3=0	0×4=0	0×5=0
1×0=0	1×1=1	1×2=2	1×3=3	1×4=4	1×5=5
2×0=0	2×1=2	2×2=4	2×3=6	2×4=8	2×5=10
3×0=0	3×1=3	3×2=6	3×3=9	3×4=12	3×5=15
4×0=0	4×1=4	4×2=8	4×3=12	4×4=16	4×5=20
5×0=0	5×1=5	5×2=10	5×3=15	5×4=20	5×5=25
6×0=0	6×1=6	6×2=12	6×3=18	6×4=24	6×5=30
7×0=0	7×1=7	7×2=14	7×3=21	7×4=28	7×5=35
8×0=0	8×1=8	8×2=16	8×3=24	8×4=32	8×5=40
9×0=0	9×1=9	9×2=18	9×3=27	9×4=36	9×5=45
10×0=0	10×1=10	10×2=20	10×3=30	10×4=40	10×5=50

Go back to the grid on page six and look at the array of numbers.
Do the patterns make sense?

$0 \times 6 = 0$	$0 \times 7 = 0$	$0 \times 8 = 0$	$0 \times 9 = 0$	$0 \times 10 = 0$
$1 \times 6 = 6$	$1 \times 7 = 7$	$1 \times 8 = 8$	$1 \times 9 = 9$	$1 \times 10 = 10$
$2 \times 6 = 12$	$2 \times 7 = 14$	$2 \times 8 = 16$	$2 \times 9 = 18$	$2 \times 10 = 20$
$3 \times 6 = 18$	$3 \times 7 = 21$	$3 \times 8 = 24$	$3 \times 9 = 27$	$3 \times 10 = 30$
$4 \times 6 = 24$	$4 \times 7 = 28$	$4 \times 8 = 32$	$4 \times 9 = 36$	$4 \times 10 = 40$
$5 \times 6 = 30$	$5 \times 7 = 35$	$5 \times 8 = 40$	$5 \times 9 = 45$	$5 \times 10 = 50$
$6 \times 6 = 36$	$6 \times 7 = 42$	$6 \times 8 = 48$	$6 \times 9 = 54$	$6 \times 10 = 60$
$7 \times 6 = 42$	$7 \times 7 = 49$	$7 \times 8 = 56$	$7 \times 9 = 63$	$7 \times 10 = 70$
$8 \times 6 = 48$	$8 \times 7 = 56$	$8 \times 8 = 64$	$8 \times 9 = 72$	$8 \times 10 = 80$
$9 \times 6 = 54$	$9 \times 7 = 63$	$9 \times 8 = 72$	$9 \times 9 = 81$	$9 \times 10 = 90$
$10 \times 6 = 60$	$10 \times 7 = 70$	$10 \times 8 = 80$	$10 \times 9 = 90$	$10 \times 10 = 100$

2×2=4

When you create
a picture using
small pieces of stone,
wood, tiles, or glass,
it is called a mosaic.

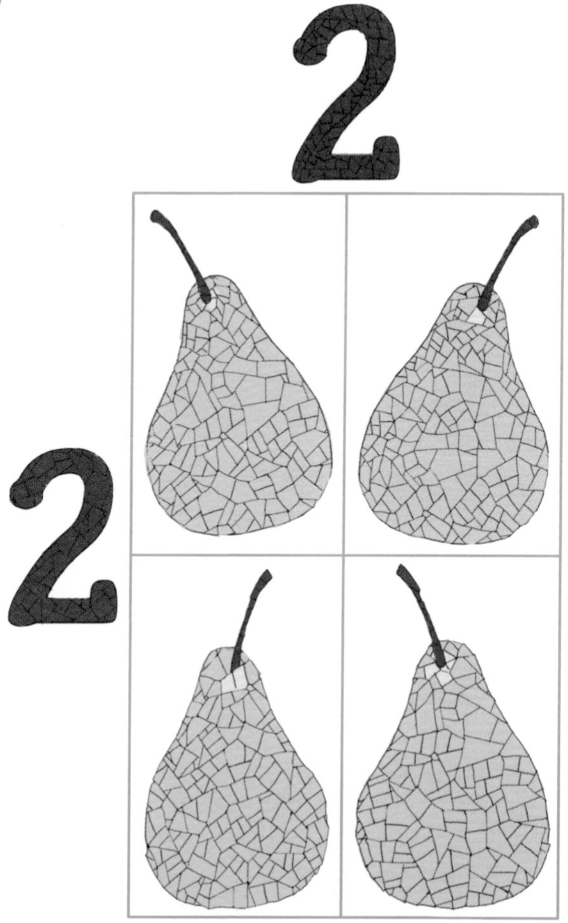

2

2

Now let's look at the equation and grid on this page.
Two times two equals four.

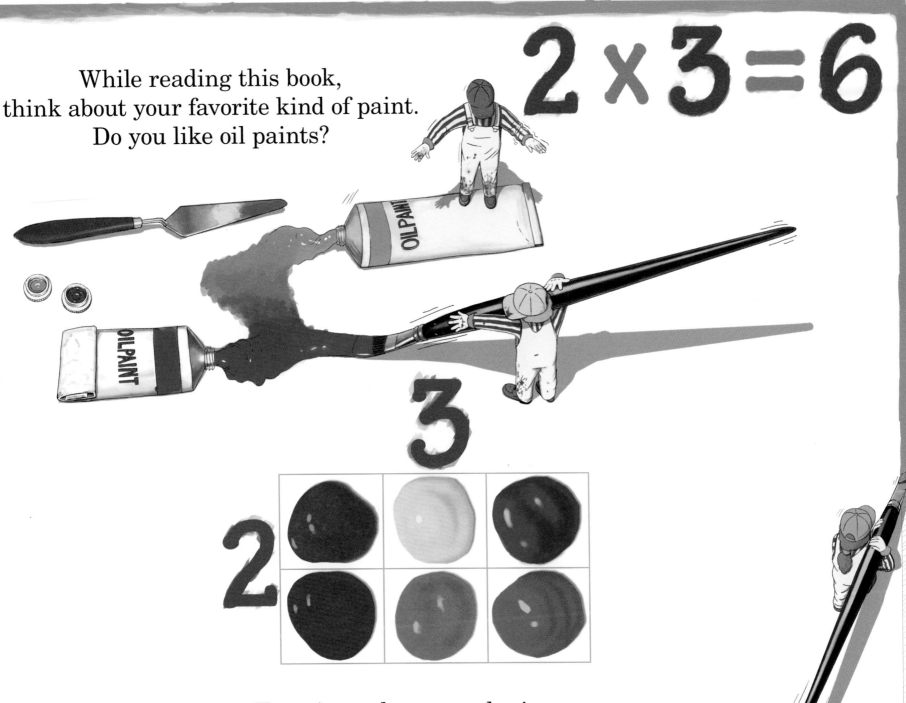

While reading this book,
think about your favorite kind of paint.
Do you like oil paints?

$$2 \times 3 = 6$$

Two times three equals six.
What type of arithmetic is your favorite?
Is it multiplication, addition, subtraction, or division?

2 × 4 = 8

The kids are covered with soot because it is messy, but fun, to draw with charcoal.

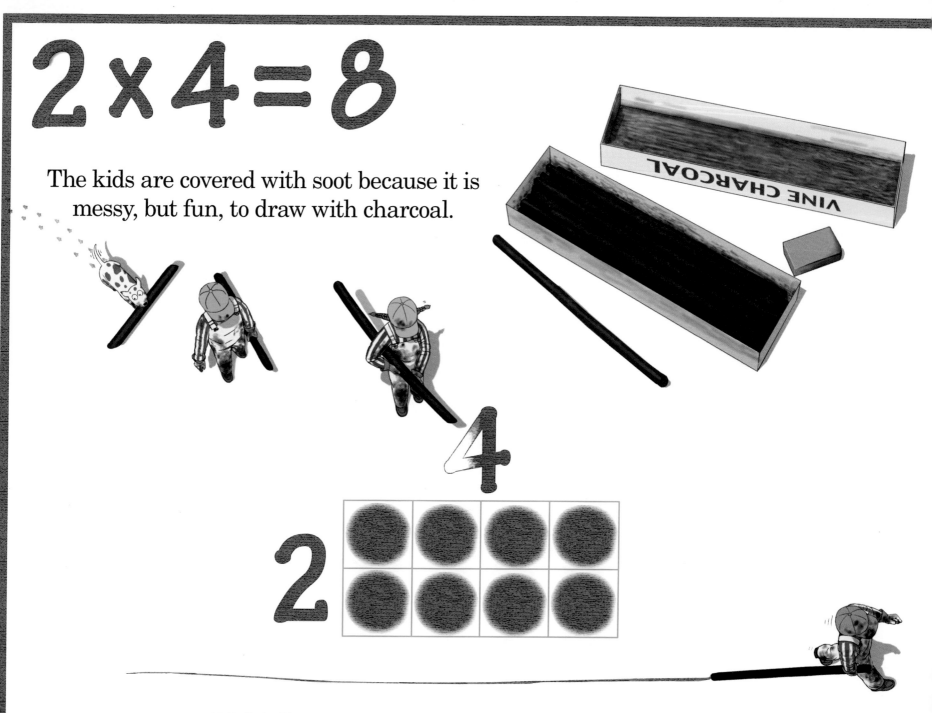

Multiplication is a quick way to add equal numbers.
Two times four is the same as two plus two plus two plus two.
They both equal eight.

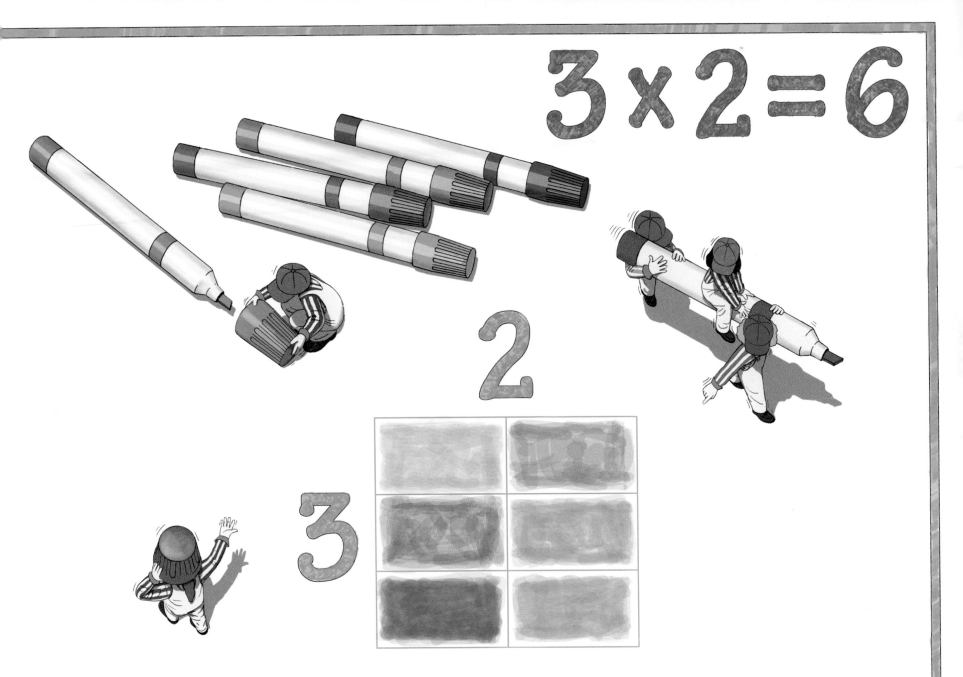

Three times two equals six. Counting by threes is the same as learning the "threes" multiplication table. Three, six, nine, twelve, fifteen, eighteen, twenty-one, twenty-four, twenty-seven, thirty—keep on counting while drawing with the markers.
For fun, follow the "threes" column or row on the page six grid.

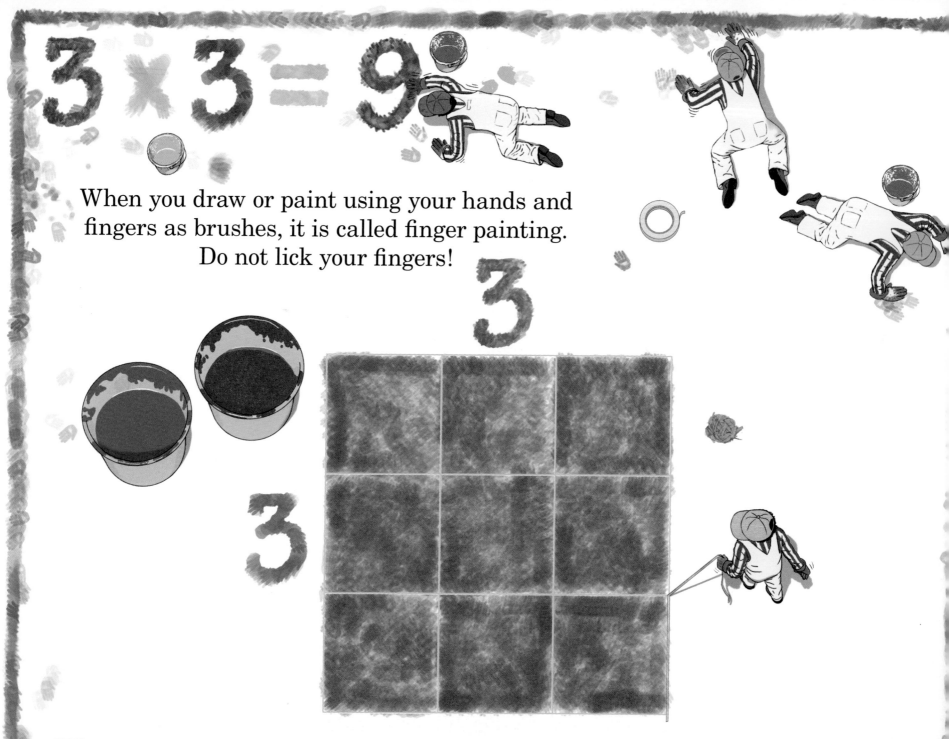

3 × 3 = 9

When you draw or paint using your hands and fingers as brushes, it is called finger painting. Do not lick your fingers!

3

3

When a number is multiplied by itself, the product is called a square number. Three times three equals nine.

SQUARE NUMBERS

The products shown below are square numbers.
The grid showing the equation is square.
Now you know where the math term "square number" comes from.

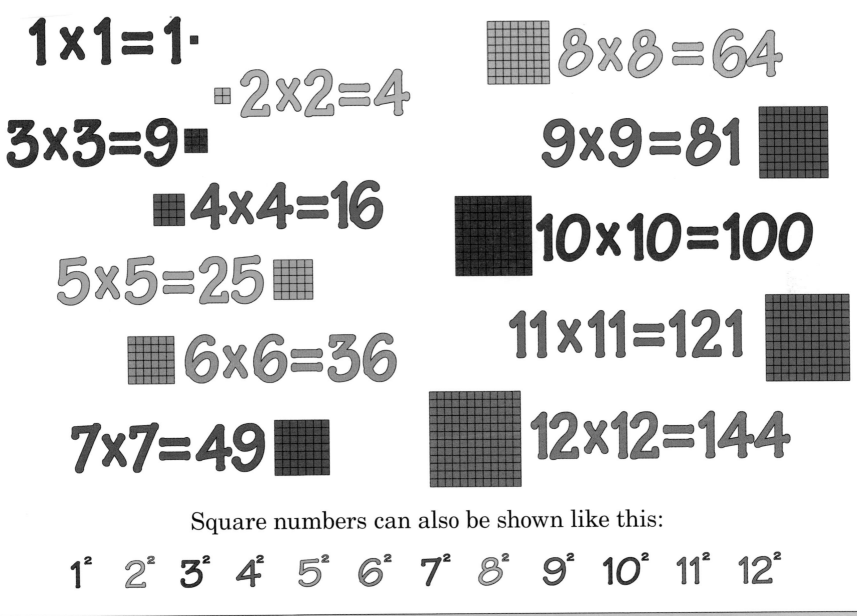

$1 \times 1 = 1$·

$2 \times 2 = 4$

$3 \times 3 = 9$

$4 \times 4 = 16$

$5 \times 5 = 25$

$6 \times 6 = 36$

$7 \times 7 = 49$

$8 \times 8 = 64$

$9 \times 9 = 81$

$10 \times 10 = 100$

$11 \times 11 = 121$

$12 \times 12 = 144$

Square numbers can also be shown like this:

1^2 2^2 3^2 4^2 5^2 6^2 7^2 8^2 9^2 10^2 11^2 12^2

4 x 2 = 8

The kids are silk-screening. They squeegee ink through the cloth to print the numbers. Silk-screening is often used to decorate T-shirts.

2

4

Four times two equals eight.
If you want to be really technical, the first factor is called the multiplicand, and the second factor is called the multiplier.

$$4 \times 3 = 12$$

The kids are now making a collage with scissors, glue, old newspapers, and magazines.

Think of all the factors that can be multiplied to make the product twelve.

$1 \times 12 = 12 \qquad 12 \times 1 = 12 \qquad 2 \times 6 = 12 \qquad 6 \times 2 = 12 \qquad 3 \times 4 = 12 \qquad 4 \times 3 = 12$

One, two, three, four, six, and twelve are all factors of twelve.

4 x 4 = 16

Do not be confused by the linoleum cuts.
Ink is applied on a backward design
and then printed in reverse.

Four times four equals sixteen. Sixteen is a square number. If someone asks you,
"What is the square root of sixteen?" the answer is four.
You will learn about square roots in division.

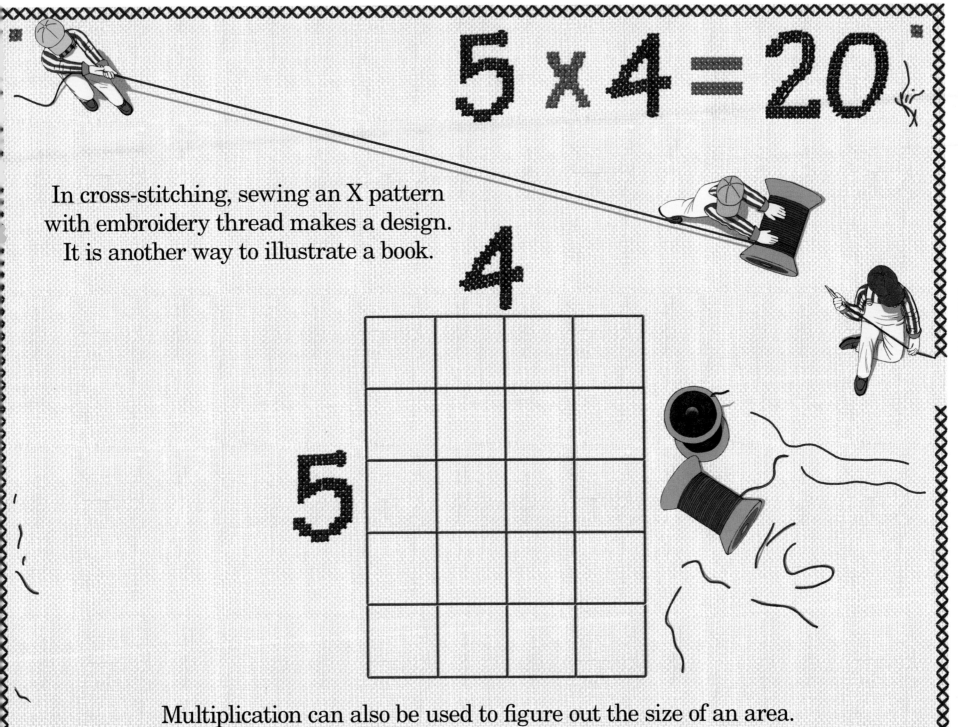

5 x 4 = 20

In cross-stitching, sewing an X pattern
with embroidery thread makes a design.
It is another way to illustrate a book.

4

5

Multiplication can also be used to figure out the size of an area.
This is a grid of twenty sections. Five sections times four equal twenty sections.
Remember, in multiplication, the letter X is used as a times sign.

6 × 4 = 24

Writing multiplication facts with sidewalk chalk is a great way to practice your math.

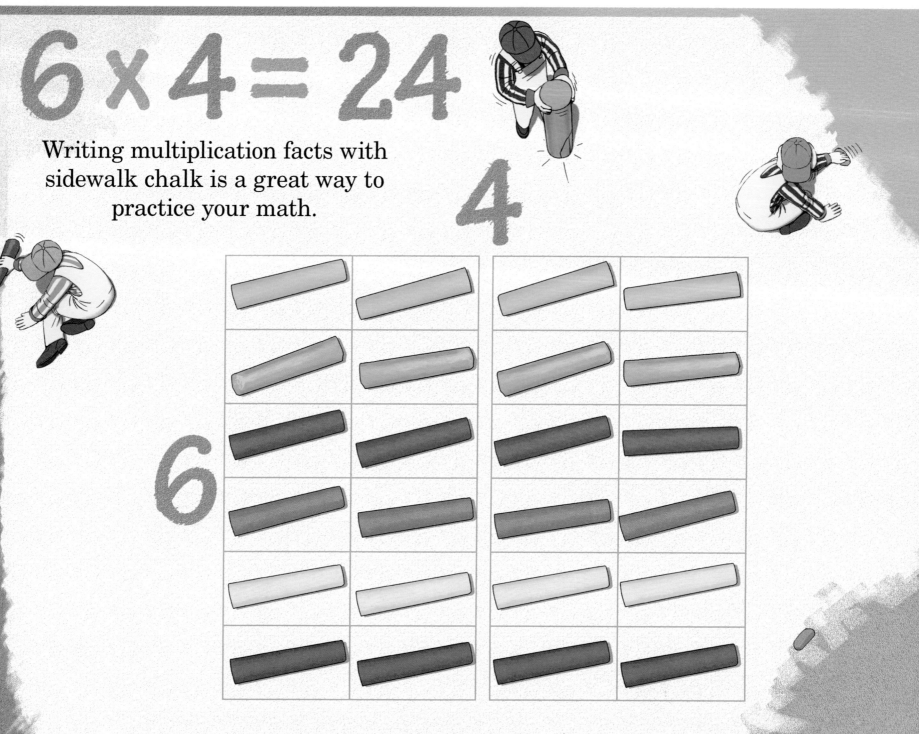

This time we used two twelve-section grids next to each other.
We now have six times four equals twenty-four.

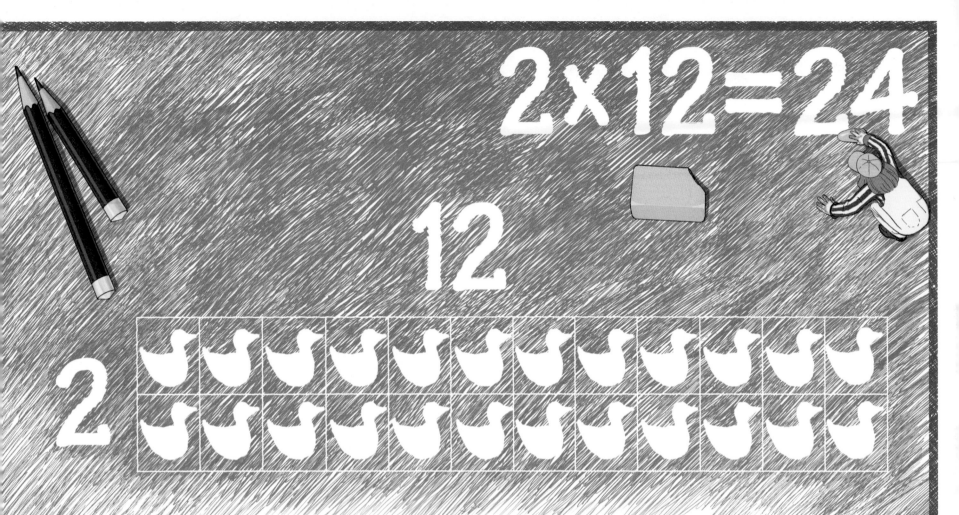

$$2 \times 12 = 24$$

After covering the page with pencil,
you can draw with erasers. Cool!

Quick—without counting, how many ducks are here?
You can get the answer by doing multiplication.
Two times twelve equals twenty-four. Quack!

10 x 12 = 120

Tap. Tap. Tap. The kids are hanging up their artwork.

12

10

12 SHEETS
12 SHEETS
12 SHEETS
12 SHEETS
12 SHEETS
12 SHEETS
12 SHEETS
12 SHEETS
12 SHEETS
12 SHEETS

It would take forever to count all of the poster board in these ten packages. Ten times twelve equals one hundred and twenty. Multiplication makes it easy.

$$4 \times 10 = 40$$

The kids are arranging the mobiles.

$$40 \times 12 = 480$$

There are 480 sheets of poster board in the packages on this page.

12 SHEETS	12 SHEETS	12 SHEETS	12 SHEETS
12 SHEETS	12 SHEETS	12 SHEETS	12 SHEETS
12 SHEETS	12 SHEETS	12 SHEETS	12 SHEETS
12 SHEETS	12 SHEETS	12 SHEETS	12 SHEETS
12 SHEETS	12 SHEETS	12 SHEETS	12 SHEETS
12 SHEETS	12 SHEETS	12 SHEETS	12 SHEETS
12 SHEETS	12 SHEETS	12 SHEETS	12 SHEETS
12 SHEETS	12 SHEETS	12 SHEETS	12 SHEETS
12 SHEETS	12 SHEETS	12 SHEETS	12 SHEETS
12 SHEETS	12 SHEETS	12 SHEETS	12 SHEETS

The associative property of multiplication allows you to do the math two ways.
First, try $4 \times 10 = 40$ and then $40 \times 12 = 480$.
Or do it like this: $4 \times$ the product of 10×12. $10 \times 12 = 120$.
$4 \times 120 = 480$. The answer is the same.